THE CONSTELLATION COLLECTION

ORION

Amy B. Rogers

PowerKiDS
press.

New York

Published in 2016 by The Rosen Publishing Group, Inc.
29 East 21st Street, New York, NY 10010

First Edition

Editor: Katie Kawa
Book Design: Katelyn Heinle

Photo Credits: Cover, p. 5 Yganko/Shutterstock.com; back cover, p. 1 nienora/Shutterstock.com; p. 7 http://upload.wikimedia.org/wikipedia/commons/4/45/Orion_constellation_Hevelius.jpg; p. 8 angelinast/Shutterstock.com; p. 9 muuraa/Shutterstock.com; p. 11 David Nunuk/All Canada Photos/Getty Images; p. 13 David Herraez Calzada/Shutterstock.com; p. 15 http://upload.wikimedia.org/wikipedia/commons/6/68/Barnard_33.jpg; p. 17 Alan Dyer/Stocktrek Images/Getty Images; p. 18 Astrobobo/Shutterstock.com; p. 19 © iStockphoto.com/Rastan; p. 21 peresanz/Thinkstock.com; p. 22 Alan Dyer/Visuals Unlimited, Inc./Getty Images.

Library of Congress Cataloging-in-Publication Data

Rogers, Amy B.
Orion / by Amy B. Rogers.
p. cm. — (The constellation collection)
Includes index.
ISBN 978-1-4994-0933-8 (pbk.)
ISBN 978-1-4994-0956-7 (6 pack)
ISBN 978-1-4994-0990-1 (library binding)
1. Orion (Constellation) — Juvenile literature. 2. Stars — Formation — Juvenile literature. I. Rogers, Amy B. II. Title.
QB802.R58 2016
523.8—d23

CONTENTS

THE HUNTER

It's fun to look for shapes in the stars! Groups of stars that form the shapes of people, animals, and other objects are called constellations. Orion, which is also called the Hunter, is one of the easiest constellations to find in the night sky. It can be found by looking for three bright stars that make a straight line. This straight line is Orion's belt.

The rest of this constellation can be seen by looking around the belt. Lines of stars make up the outline of Orion's body, arms, club, and **shield**. Two stars below the belt are his feet.

STAR STORY
Orion is most easily seen in winter.

THE LINE OF THREE FAINTER STARS BELOW ORION'S BELT IS HIS SWORD.

DIFFERENT CULTURES, DIFFERENT STORIES

Many groups of people throughout history created **myths** to explain how a hunter ended up in the stars. Orion got its name from a hunter in an ancient Greek myth. According to one Greek myth, Artemis, who was the goddess of hunting, fell in love with Orion. However, her brother Apollo tricked her into shooting Orion with an arrow, which killed him. Artemis then put Orion in the stars.

Even before the ancient Greeks created their Orion myths, other **cultures** were telling stories about this constellation. The ancient Egyptians and Sumerians both had their own myths to explain Orion.

STAR STORY
The Sumerians called this constellation Uru-anna, which means "light of heaven."

SOME MYTHS STATED THAT ORION WAS KILLED FOR BRAGGING ABOUT HIS HUNTING SKILLS.

ORION AND SCORPIUS

Many cultures have myths that connect Orion to the constellation Scorpius, or the Scorpion. In fact, in several versions of the Orion myth, Orion was actually stung to death by a scorpion.

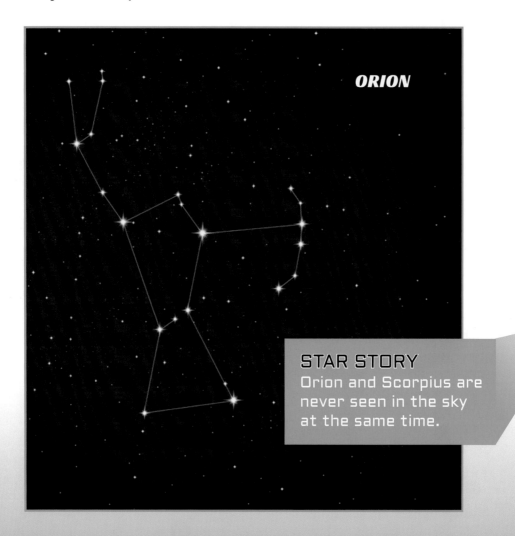

ORION

STAR STORY
Orion and Scorpius are never seen in the sky at the same time.

In some myths, Orion chases Scorpius in the sky. In others, he's hiding from Scorpius. These myths were created to explain why one constellation rises in the sky during the year as the other one sets. While Orion is a winter constellation, Scorpius is best seen in summer. Both Orion and Scorpius are known for being bright and easy to find in the sky.

SCORPIUS

THE CONSTELLATION SCORPIUS IS SOMETIMES CALLED SCORPIO.

WHERE DO STARS COME FROM?

All constellations, including Orion, are made up of stars that were born and will one day die. A star is born within a cloud of gas and dust in space, which is called a nebula. Over time, the pull of **gravity** within the nebula becomes so strong that the cloud begins to **collapse**. The gas and dust become packed together to form the core, or center, of the star.

As the nebula collapses, the gas and dust get hotter. Eventually, the core gets hot enough to produce a **reaction** called nuclear fusion. At this point, the gas and dust become a star.

STAR STORY

Nuclear fusion happens when two or more **atoms** join together to form a heavier atom. This reaction lets out large amounts of heat and light.

WHEN NEBULAE BEGIN TO COLLAPSE, THEY'RE CALLED PROTOSTARS.

THE ORION NEBULA

You can see nebulae in the sky on a clear night. In fact, some nebulae can be seen in the Orion constellation. One of these nebulae is called the Orion Nebula or the Great Orion Nebula.

The Orion Nebula is found below the constellation's belt of stars. It looks like a fuzzy patch of light around one of the stars that form Orion's sword. This nebula is an emission nebula, which means it's a place where stars are born. The Orion Nebula is the closest emission nebula to Earth.

STAR STORY
The Orion Nebula is the only emission, or star-making, nebula we can see with just our eyes.

THE ORION NEBULA IS ONE OF THE MOST FAMOUS NEBULAE IN THE UNIVERSE.

A HORSE IN THE SKY!

Another famous nebula that can be seen in Orion is the Horsehead Nebula. This nebula got its name from the fact that it's curved in a way that looks like a horse's head. It's one of the easiest nebulae to recognize because of its shape.

The Horsehead Nebula is a dark nebula. This means it's a very dense cloud of dust and gas. Dark nebulae can be seen because of the brightness of the stars around them. Scientists believe one of the stars in Orion, which is named Sigma Orionis, lights up the sky around the Horsehead Nebula. This is how we can see the nebula.

STAR STORY

The Horsehead Nebula was discovered in 1888 by Williamina Fleming, a Scottish **astronomer** working at the Harvard College Observatory.

DARK NEBULAE, SUCH AS THE HORSEHEAD NEBULA, LOOK LIKE A DARK SPOT IN THE SKY AGAINST THE BRIGHT BACKGROUND OF THE STARS.

SUPERGIANT STARS

Orion is known for the nebulae that can be seen in it. It's also known as the home of two famously bright stars: Rigel and Betelgeuse. These stars help make Orion the brightest constellation in the sky.

Both Rigel and Betelgeuse are kinds of stars known as supergiants. These are the largest stars in the universe. Supergiants burn more quickly than smaller stars, which means they have shorter lives. Both Rigel and Betelgeuse are much larger than the sun. They don't look as large to people on Earth because they're much farther away.

STAR STORY
Betelgeuse is also known as Alpha Orionis, and Rigel is Beta Orionis.

BETELGEUSE

RIGEL AND BETELGEUSE ARE EASY TO FIND IN ORION. ONE IS AT THE TOP OF THE CONSTELLATION, AND THE OTHER IS AT THE BOTTOM.

RIGEL

THE BRIGHTEST STAR

Rigel is the brightest star in Orion. Its name means "the left leg of the giant," which refers to its place at the bottom of Orion's body, below the line of stars that form the belt.

Rigel has two companion stars very close to it. These two stars, which are known as Rigel B and Rigel C, are a double star. A double star is a pair of stars that are so close in the sky they look like they could be one star. These stars orbit, or circle, around a shared center of gravity.

RIGEL

STAR STORY
Rigel gives off almost 50,000 times more light than the sun!

DOUBLE STARS, SUCH AS RIGEL B AND RIGEL C, ARE SOMETIMES CALLED BINARY STAR SYSTEMS. THEY'RE BEST SEEN THROUGH A TELESCOPE, WHICH IS A DEVICE BUILT TO MAKE SPACE OBJECTS APPEAR LARGER.

THE GIANT'S SHOULDER

Betelgeuse is the second-brightest star in Orion, but it's best known for being one of the largest known stars in the universe. It's around 950 times larger than the sun!

Betelgeuse is a variable star. This means its brightness changes as its **atmosphere** grows and shrinks. Betelgeuse goes through a cycle of changes in brightness every six years. Scientists also believe this star is shrinking as it gets older. Betelgeuse is around 8.5 million years old, and it could die at any time. Because it's so large, it will die with a huge explosion that people will see from Earth!

STAR STORY
Betelgeuse's name means "the giant's shoulder."

BETELGEUSE

ORION

BETELGEUSE IS KNOWN FOR ITS DEEP REDDISH COLOR. IT CAN BE FOUND NEAR THE TOP OF ORION'S BODY.

WATCHING THE WINTER SKY

Orion is one of the most famous constellations in the sky. It's home to nebulae where new stars are born. It's also home to two of the brightest and biggest stars studied by astronomers.

The winter sky is filled with cool constellations to find. Once you find Orion, you can find Taurus, which is also known as the Bull. You can also find Gemini, or the Twins, by looking for two bright stars above Betelgeuse. The next time you go outside on a clear winter night, look up at the stars. Can you find Orion?

GLOSSARY

astronomer: A person who studies stars, planets, and other objects in outer space.

atmosphere: The gases that surround a planet or star.

atom: A tiny bit of matter. Everything that exists is made of atoms.

collapse: To fall together.

culture: The beliefs and ways of life of a certain group of people.

gravity: The natural force that causes planets and stars to move toward each other.

myth: A story told in ancient cultures to explain a practice, belief, or part of nature.

reaction: A change or response.

shield: A large piece of metal or wood carried by someone to keep them safe.

INDEX

WEBSITES

Due to the changing nature of Internet links, PowerKids Press has developed an online list of websites related to the subject of this book. This site is updated regularly. Please use this link to access the list: www.powerkidslinks.com/tcc/ori